Grandma's Story

Grandma's Story

TRINH T. MINH-HA

Published in 2025 by Spiral House, an imprint of Silver Press.

'Grandma's Story' by Trinh T. Minh-ha was first published in *Woman, Native, Other*, Indiana University Press, 1989. Reprinted by permission of the publisher.

ISBN-13: 978-1-0685918-0-8

Design by Rose Nordin
Typeset in Adobe Caslon Pro by Jay Drinkall
Printed and bound in the UK by CPI

EU GPSR Authorised Representative: Logos Europe, 9 rue Nicolas Poussin, 17000, La Rochelle, France.
contact@logoseurope.eu

1 3 5 7 9 10 8 6 4 2

Contents

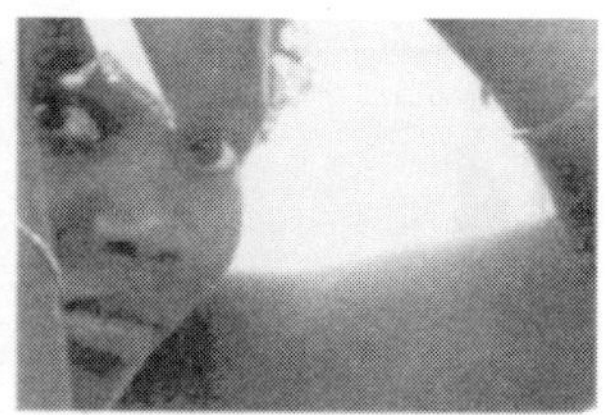
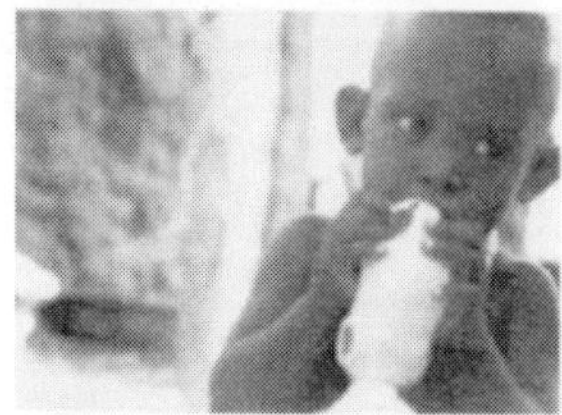

'Reassemblage. From silences to silences, the fragile essence of each fragment sparks across the screen, subsides, and takes flight. Almost there half named.'

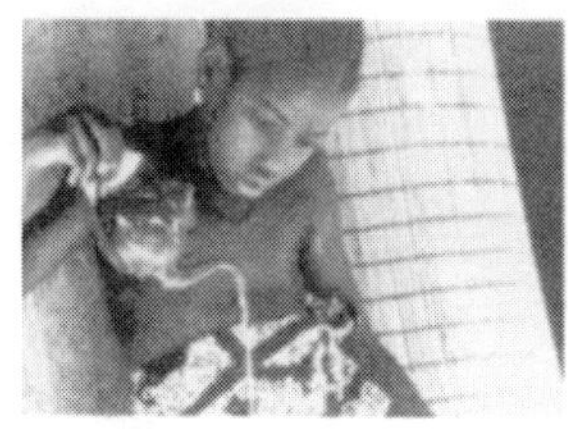
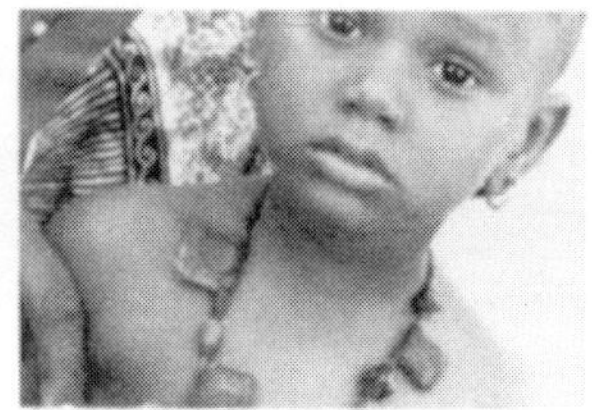

See all things howsoever they flourish
Return to the root from which they grew
This return to the root is called Quietness
– Lao Tzu, *Tao-te-ching*, 16 (tr. A. Waley)

Truth and fact: story and history

Let me tell you a story. For all I have is a story. Story passed on from generation to generation, named Joy. Told for the joy it gives the storyteller and the listener. Joy inherent in the process of storytelling. Whoever understands it also understands that a story, as distressing as it can be in its joy, never takes anything away from anybody. Its name, remember, is Joy. Its double, Woe Morrow Show.

Let the one who is diseuse, one who is mother who waits nine days and nine nights be found. Restore memory. Let the one who is

> diseuse, one who is daughter restore spring with her each appearance from beneath the earth. The ink spills thickest before it runs dry before it stops writing at all. (Theresa Hak Kyung Cha)[1]

Something must be said. Must be said that has not been *and* has been said before. 'It will take a long time, but the story must be told. There must not be any lies' (Leslie Marmon Silko). It will take a long time for living cannot be told, not merely told: living is not livable. Understanding, however, is creating, and living, such an immense gift that thousands of people benefit from each past or present life being lived. The story depends upon every one of us to come into being. It needs us all, needs our remembering, understanding, and creating what we have heard together to keep on coming into being. The story of a people. Of us, peoples. Story, history, literature (or religion, philosophy, natural science, ethics) – all in one. They call it the tool of primitive man, the simplest vehicle of truth. When history separated itself from story, it started indulging in accumulation and facts. Or it thought it could. It thought it could build up to History because the Past, unrelated to the Present and the Future, is lying there in its entirety, waiting to be revealed and related. The act of revealing bears in itself a magical (not factual) quality – inherited undoubtedly from 'primitive' storytelling –

for the Past perceived as such is a well-organized past whose organization is already given. Managing to identify with History, history (with a small letter h) thus manages to oppose the factual to the fictional (turning a blind eye to the 'magicality' of its claims); the story-writer – the historian – to the storyteller. As long as the transformation, manipulations, or redistributions inherent in the collecting of events are overlooked, the division continues its course, as sure of its itinerary as it certainly dreams to be. Story-writing becomes history-writing, and history quickly sets itself apart, consigning story to the realm of tale, legend, myth, fiction, literature. Then, since fictional and factual have come to a point where they mutually exclude each other, fiction, not infrequently, means lies, and fact, truth. DID IT REALLY HAPPEN? IS IT A TRUE STORY?

> I don't want to listen to any more of your stories [Maxine Hong Kingston screamed at her champion-story-talker mother]; they have no logic. They scramble me up. You lie with stories. You won't tell me a story and then say, 'This is a true story', or 'This is just a story.' I can't tell the difference. I don't even know what your real names are. I can't tell what's real and what you made up.[2]

Which truth? the question unavoidably arises. The story has been defined as 'a free narration, not necessarily factual but truthful in character . . . [It] gives us human nature in its bold outlines; history, in its individual details.'[3] Truth. Not one but two: truth and fact, just like in the old times when queens were born and kings were made in Egypt. (Queens and princesses were then 'Royal Mothers' from birth, whereas the king wore the crown of high priest and did not receive the Horus-name until his coronation.) Poetry, Aristotle said, is truer than history. Storytelling as literature (narrative poetry) must then be truer than history. If we rely on history to tell us what happened at a specific time and place, we can rely on the story to tell us not only what might have happened, but also what is happening at an unspecified time and place. No wonder that in old tales storytellers are very often women, witches, and prophets. The African *griot* and *griotte* are well known for being poet, storyteller, historian, musician, and magician – all at once. But why truth at all? Why this battle for truth and on behalf of truth? I do not remember having asked grandmother once whether the story she was telling me was true or not. Neither do I recall her asking me whether the story I was reading her was true or not. We knew we could make each other cry, laugh, or fear, but we never thought of saying to each other, 'This is just a story.' A story is a story. There was no need for clarification – a need many adults considered 'natural' or imperative among children – for there was no such thing as 'a blind acceptance of the story as literally true'. Perhaps the story has become *just* a story when I have become adept at consuming truth as fact. Imagination is thus equated with falsification, and I am made to believe that if, accordingly, I am not told or do not establish in so many words what is true and what is false, I or the listener may no longer be able to differentiate fancy from fact (sic). Literature and history once were/still are stories: this does not necessarily mean that the space they form is undifferentiated, but that this space can articulate on a different set of principles, one which may be said to stand outside the hierarchical realm of facts. On the one hand, each society has its own politics of truth; on the other hand, being truthful is being in the in-between of all regimes of truth. Outside specific time, outside specialized space: 'Truth embraces with it all other abstentions other than itself' (Theresa Hak Kyung Cha).

Keepers and transmitters

Truth is when it is itself no longer. Diseuse, Thought-Woman, Spider-Woman, *griotte*, storytalker, fortune-teller, witch. If you have the patience to listen, she will take delight in relating it to you. An entire history, an entire vision of the world, a lifetime story. Mother always has a mother. And Great Mothers are recalled as the goddesses of all waters, the sources of diseases and of healing, the protectresses of women and of childbearing. To listen carefully is to preserve. But to preserve is to burn, for understanding means creating.

> Let the one who is diseuse. Diseuse de bonne aventure. Let her call forth. Let her break open the spell cast upon time upon time again and again. (Theresa Hak Kyung Cha)[4]

The world's earliest archives or libraries were the memories of women. Patiently transmitted from mouth to ear, body to body, hand to hand. In the process of storytelling, speaking and listening refer to realities that do not involve just the imagination. The speech is seen, heard, smelled, tasted, and touched. It destroys, brings into life, nurtures. Every woman partakes in the chain of guardianship and of transmission. In Africa it is said that every *griotte* who dies is a whole library that burns down (a 'library in which the archives are not classified but are completely inventoried' [A. Hampaté Bâ]). Phrases like 'I sucked it at my mother's breast' or 'I have it from Our Mother' to express what has been passed down by the elders are common in this part of the world. Tell me and let me tell my hearers what I have heard from you who heard it from your mother and your grandmother, so that what is said may be guarded and unfailingly transmitted to the women of tomorrow, who will be our children and the children of our children. These are the opening lines she used to chant before embarking on a story. I owe that to you, her and her, who owe it to her, her and her. I memorize, recognize, and name my source(s), not to validate my voice through the voice of an authority (for we, women, have little authority in the History of Literature, and wise women never draw their powers from authority), but to evoke her and sing. The bond between women and word. Among women themselves. To produce their full effect, words must, indeed, be chanted rhythmically, in cadences, off cadences.

> My great-grandmama told my grandmama the part she lived through that my grandmama didn't live through and my grandmama told my mama what they both lived through and my mama told me what they all lived through and we were supposed to pass it down like that from generation to generation so we'd never forget. Even though they'd burned everything to play like it didn't ever happen. (Gayl Jones)[5]

In this chain and continuum, I am but one link. The story is me, neither me nor mine. It does not really belong to me, and while I feel greatly responsible for it, I also enjoy the irresponsibility of the pleasure obtained through the process of transferring. Pleasure in the copy, pleasure in the reproduction. No repetition can ever be identical, but my story carries with it their stories, their history, and our story repeats itself endlessly despite our persistence in denying it. *I don't believe it. That story could not happen today.* Then someday our children will speak about us here present, about those days when things like that could happen . . . :

> It was like I didn't know how much was me and Mutt and how much was Great Gram and Corregidora – like Mama when she had started talking like Great Gram. But was what Corregidora had done to *her*, to *them*, any worse than what Mutt had done to me, than what we had done to each other, than what Mama had done to Daddy, or what he had done to her in return . . . (Gayl Jones)[6]

> Upon seeing her you know how it was for her. You know how it might have been. You recline, you lapse, you fall, you see before you what you have seen before. Repeated, without your even knowing it. It is you standing there. It is you waiting outside in the summer day. (Theresa Hak Kyung Cha)[7]

Every gesture, every word involves our past, present, and future. The body never stops accumulating, and years and years have gone by mine without my being able to stop them, stop it. My sympathies and grudges appear at the same time familiar and unfamiliar to me; I dwell in them, they dwell in me, and we dwell in each other, more as guest than as owner. My story, no doubt, is me, but it is also, no doubt, older than me.

Younger than me, older than the humanized. Unmeasurable, uncontainable, so immense that it exceeds all attempts at humanizing. But humanizing we do, and also overdo, for the vision of a story that has no end – no end, no middle, no beginning; no start, no stop, no progression; neither backward nor forward, only a stream that flows into another stream, an open sea – is the vision of a madwoman. 'The unleashed tides of muteness', as Clarice Lispector puts it. We fear heights, we fear the headless, the bottomless, the boundless. And we are in terror of letting ourselves be engulfed by the depths of muteness. This is why we keep on doing violence to words: to tame and cook the wild-raw, to adopt the vertiginously infinite. Truth does not make sense; it exceeds meaning and exceeds measure. It exceeds all regimes of truth. So, when we insist on telling over and over again, we insist on repetition in re-creation (and vice versa). On distributing the story into smaller proportions that will correspond to the capacity of absorption of our mouths, the capacity of vision of our eyes, and the capacity of bearing of our bodies. Each story is at once a fragment and a whole; a whole within a whole. And the same story has always been changing, for things which do not shift and grow cannot continue to circulate. Dead. Dead times, dead words, dead tongues. Not to repeat in oblivion.

Sediment. Turned stone. Let the one who is diseuse dust breathe away the distance of the well. Let the one who is diseuse again sit upon the stone nine days and nine nights. thus. Making stand again, Eleusis. (Theresa Hak Kyung Cha)[8]

Storytelling in the 'civilized' context

The simplest vehicle of truth, the story is also said to be 'a phase of communication', 'the natural form for revealing life'. Its fascination may be explained by its power both to give a vividly felt insight into the life of other people and to revive or keep alive the forgotten, dead-ended, turned-into-stone parts of ourselves. To the wo/man of the West who spends time recording and arranging the 'data' concerning storytelling as well as 'the many rules and taboos connected with it', this tool of primitive wo/man has provided primitive peoples with opportunities 'to train their speech, formulate opinions, and express themselves' (Anna Birgitta Rooth). It gives 'a sympathetic understanding of their limitations in knowledge, and an appreciation of our privileges in civilization, due largely to the struggles of the past' (Clark W. Hetherington). It informs of the explanations they invented for 'the things [they] did not understand', and represents their religion, 'a religion growing out of fear of the unknown' (Katherine Dunlap Cather). In summary, the story is either a mere practice of the art of rhetoric or 'a repository of obsolete customs' (A. Skinner). It is mainly valued for its artistic potential and for the 'religious beliefs' or 'primitive-mind'-revealing superstitions mirrored by its content. (Like the supernatural, is the superstitious another product of the Western mind? For to accept even temporarily Cather's view on primitive religion, one is bound to ask: which [institutionalized] religion does not grow out of fear of the unknown?) Associated with backwardness, ignorance, and illiteracy, storytelling in the more 'civilized' context is therefore relegated to the realm of children. 'The fact that the story is the product of primitive man', wrote Herman H. Horne, 'explains in part why the children hunger so for the story'.[9] 'Wherever there is no written language, wherever the people are too unlettered to read what is written', Cather equally remarked, 'they still believe the legends. They love to hear them told and retold . . . As it is with unlettered peasants today, as it was with tribesmen in primitive times and with the great in medieval castle halls, it still is with the child.'[10] Primitive means elementary, therefore infantile. No wonder then that in the West storytelling is treasured above all for its educational force in the kindergarten and primary school. The mission of the storyteller, we thus hear, is to 'teach children the tales their *fathers* knew', to mold ideals, and to 'illuminate facts'. For children to gain 'right feelings' and to 'think true', the story as a pedagogical tool must inform so as to keep their opinion 'abreast of the scientific truth of the time, instead of dragging along in the superstitions of the past'. But for the story to be well-told information, it must be related 'in as fascinating a form as [in] the old myths and fables'.[11] Patch up the content of the new and the form of the old, or impose one on the other. The dis-ease lingers on. With (traditional but non-superstitious?) formulas like 'once upon a time' and 'long, long ago', the storyteller can be reasonably sure of making 'a good beginning'. For many people truth has the connotation of uniformity and prescription. Thinking true means thinking in conformity with a certain scientific (read 'scientistic') discourse produced by certain institutions. Not only has the 'civilized' mind classified many of the realities it does not understand in the categories of the untrue and the superstitious, it has also turned the story – as total event of a community, a people – into a *fatherly* lesson for children of a certain age. Indeed, in the 'civilized' context, only children are allowed to indulge in the so-called fantastic or the fantastic-true. They are perceived as belonging to a world apart, one which adults (compassionately) control and populate with toys – that is to say, with false human beings (dolls), false animals, false objects (imitative, diminutive versions of the 'real'). 'Civilized' adults fabricate, structure, and segregate the children's world; they invent toys for the latter to *play* with and stories of a specially adapted, more digestive kind to absorb, yet they insist on molding this world according to the scientifically true – the real, obviously not in its full scale, but in a reduced scale: that which is supposed to be the (God-like) child's scale. Stories, especially 'primitive-why stories' or fairy tales, must be carefully sorted and graded, for children should neither be 'deceived' nor 'duped' and 'there should never be any doubt in [their] mind as to what is make-believe and what is real'. In other words, the difference 'civilized' adults recognize in the little people's world is a mere matter of scale. The forms of constraint that rule these bigger people's world and allow them to distinguish with certainty the false from the true must, unquestionably, be exactly the same as the ones that regulate the smaller people's world. The apartheid type of difference continues to operate in all spheres of 'civilized' life. There does not seem to be any possibility either as to the existence of such things as, for example, two (or more) different realms of make-believe or two (or more) different realms of truth. The 'civilized' mind is an indisputably clear-cut mind. If once upon a time people believed in the story and thought it was true, then why should it be false today? If true and false keep on changing with the times, then isn't it true that what is 'crooked thinking' today may be 'right thinking' tomorrow? What kind of people, we then wonder, walk around asking obstinately: 'Is there not danger of making liars of children by feeding them on these [fairy] stories?' What kind of people set out for northern Alaska to study storytelling among the Indians and come round to writing: 'What especially impressed me was their eagerness to make me understand. To me this eagerness became a proof of the high value they set on their stories and what they represented'?[12] What kind of people, indeed, other than the very kind for whom the story is '*just* a story'?

A regenerating force

An oracle and a bringer of joy, the storyteller is the living memory of her time, her people. She composes on life but does not lie, for composing is not imagining, fancying, or inventing. When asked, 'What is oral tradition?' an African 'traditionalist' (a term African scholars consider more accurate than the French term '*griot*' or '*griotte*', which tends to confuse traditionalists with mere public entertainers) would most likely be nonplussed. As A. Hampaté Bâ remarks, '[s/he] might reply, after a lengthy silence: "It is total knowledge," and say no more'.[13] She might or might not reply so, for what is called here 'total knowledge' is not really nameable. At least it cannot be named (so) without incurring the risk of sliding right back into one of the many slots the 'civilized' discourse of knowledge readily provides it with. The question 'What is oral tradition?' is a question-answer that needs no answer at all. Let the one who is civilized, the one who invents 'oral tradition', let him define it for himself. For 'oral' and 'written' or 'written' versus 'oral' are notions that have been as heavily invested as the notions of 'true' and 'false' have always been. (If writing, as mentioned earlier, does not express language but encompasses it, then where does the written stop? The line distinguishing societies with writing from those without writing seems most ill-defined and leaves much to be desired . . .) Living is neither oral nor written – how can the living and the lived be contained in the merely oral? Furthermore, when she composes on life she not only gives information, entertains, develops, or expands the imagination. Not only educates. Only practices a craft. 'Mind breathes mind', a civilized man wrote, 'power feels power, and absorbs it, as it were. The telling of stories refreshes the mind as a bath refreshes the body; it gives exercise to the intellect and its powers; it tests the judgment and the feelings.'[14] Man's view is always reduced to man's mind. For this is the part of himself he values most. THE MIND. The intellect and its powers. Storytelling allows the 'civilized' narrator above all to renew his mind and exercise power through his intellect. Even though the motto reads 'Think, act, and feel', his task, he believes, is to ease the passage of the story *from mind to mind*. She, however, who sets out to revive the forgotten, to survive and supersede it ('From stone. Layers. Of stone upon stone between the layers, dormant. No more' [Theresa Hak Kyung Cha]),[15] she never speaks of and cannot be content with mere matters of the mind – such as mind transmission. The storyteller has long been known as a personage of power. True, she partakes in this living heritage of power. But her powers do more than illuminate or refresh the mind. They extinguish as quickly as they set fire. They wound as easily as they soothe. And not necessarily the mind. Abraham Lincoln, accurately observed that 'the sharpness of a refusal, or the edge of a rebuke, may be blunted by an appropriate story, so as to save wounded feeling and yet serve the purpose . . . story-telling as an emollient saves me much friction and distress'.[16] Yet this is but one more among the countless functions of storytelling. Humidity, receptivity, fecundity. Again, her speech is seen, heard, smelled, tasted, and touched. Great Mother is the goddess of all waters, the protectress of women and of childbearing, the unweary sentient hearer, the healer and also the bringer of diseases. She who gives always accepts, she who wishes to preserve never fails to refresh. Regenerate.

> She was already in her mid-sixties
> when I discovered that she would listen to me
> to all my questions and speculations.
> I was only seven or eight years old then. (Leslie Marmon Silko)[17]

Salivate, secrete the words. No water, no birth, no death, no life. No speech, no song, no story, no force, no power. The entire being is engaged in the act of speaking-listening-weaving-procreating. If she does not cry she will turn into stone. Utter, weep, wet, let it flow so as to break through (it). Layers of stone amidst layers of stone. Break with her own words. The interrelation of woman, water, and word pervades African cosmogonies. Among the Dogon, for example, the process of regeneration which the eight ancestors of the Dogon people had to undergo was carried out in the waters of the womb of the female Nummo (the Nummo spirits form a male and female Pair whose essence is divine) *while she spoke* to herself and to her own sex, accompanied by the male Nummo's voice. 'The spoken Word entered into her and wound itself round her womb in a spiral of eight turns . . . the spiral of the Word gave to the womb its regenerative movement.' Of the fertilizing power of words and their transmissions through women, it is further said that:

> the first Word had been pronounced [read 'scanned'] in front of the genitalia of a woman . . . The Word finally came from the ant-hill, that is, from the mouth of the seventh Nummo [the seventh ancestor and master of speech], which is to say from a woman's genitalia.
>
> The Second Word, contained in the craft of weaving, emerged from a mouth, which was also the primordial sex organ, in which the first childbirths took place.[18]

Thus, as a wise Dogon elder (Ogotemmêli) pointed out, 'issuing from a woman's sexual part, the Word enters another sexual part, namely the ear'. (The ear is considered to be bisexual, the auricle being male and the auditory aperture, female.) From the ear, it will, continuing the cycle, go to the sexual part where it encircles the womb. African traditions conceive of speech as a gift of God/dess and a force of creation. In Fulfulde, the word for 'speech' (*haala*) has the connotation of 'giving strength', and by extension of 'making material'. Speech is the materialization, externalization, and internalization of the vibrations of forces. That is why, A. Hampaté Bâ noted, 'every manifestation of a force in any form whatever is to be regarded as its speech ... everything in the universe speaks ... If speech is strength, that is because it creates a *bond of coming-and-going* which generates *movement and rhythm* and therefore *life and action* [my italics]. This movement to and fro is symbolized by the weaver's feet going up and down ... (the symbolism of the loom is entirely based on creative speech in action).'[19] Making material: spinning and weaving is a euphonious heritage of wo/mankind handed on from generation to generation of weavers within the clapping of the shuttle and the creaking of the block – which the Dogon call 'the creaking of the Word'. 'The cloth was the Word'; the same term, *soy*, is used among the Dogon to signify both the woven material and the spoken word. Life is a perpetual to and fro, a dis/continuous releasing and absorbing of the self. Let her weave her story within their stories, her life amidst their lives. And while she weaves, let her whip, spur, and set them on fire. Thus making them sing again. Very softly a-new a-gain.

At once 'black' and 'white' magic

'The witch is a woman; the wizard is a male imitation' (Robert Briffault). In many parts of the world, magic (and witchcraft) is regarded as essentially a woman's function. It is said that 'in primitive thought every woman is credited with the possession of magic powers'. Yet she who possesses that power is always the last one to credit it. Old Lao Tzu warned: the wo/man of virtue is not virtuous; the one who never fails in virtue has no virtue at all. Practicing power for the sake of power – an idea implied in the widely assumed image of the witch as exclusively an evildoer – is an inheritance, I suspect, of the 'civilized' mind. She who brings death and disease also brings life and health. The line dividing the good and the evil, magic and witchcraft, does not always seem to be as clear-cut as it should be. In the southern Celebes, for example, 'All the deities and spirits from whom sorcerers, whether male or female, derive their power are spoken of as their "grandmothers".' Throughout Africa, priestesses are called 'Mothers', and the numerous female fetishes served exclusively by women are known as the 'Mother fetishes'. Among the Butwa, the female hierophants are named 'the mothers of the Butwa mysteries'. Among the Bir, the women are those who perform the essential ritual of maintaining the sacred fire. In Indonesia, America, northern Asia, and northern Europe, it has been demonstrated that 'magical practices and primitive priestly functions formerly belonged to the exclusive sphere of women and that they were taken up [appropriated] by men at a comparatively late epoch'. Thus, the adoption of female attire by male shamans and priests is a widespread phenomenon that still prevails in today's religious contexts. Imitating women and wearing women's clothes – priestly robes, skirts, aprons, sottanas, woven loinclothes – are regarded as bestowing greater power: the Mothers' power. [20] Of making material. Of composing on life. Her speech, her storytelling is at once magic, sorcery, and religion. It enchants. It animates, sets into motion, and rouses the forces that lie dormant in things, in beings. It is 'bewitching'. At once 'black' and 'white' magic. Which, however, causes sickness and death? which brings joy into life? For white, remember, is the color for mourning in many cultures. The same 'medicines', the same dances, the same sorcery are said to be used in both. As occasion arises, the same magic may serve for beneficent and maleficent ends. This is why her power is so dreaded; because it can be used for harm; because when it is wielded by one sex, it arouses alarm in the other. The (wizard's) game dates from the times when every practice of this art by women became a threat to men and was automatically presumed to be malignant in intention; when every magic woman must necessarily be a witch – no longer a fairy who works wonders nor a Mother-priestess-prophetess who nurtures, protects, restores, and warns against ill-will. Ill assumption leads to ill action. Men appropriate women's power of 'making material' to themselves and, not infrequently, corrupt it out of ignorance. The story becomes *just* a story. It becomes a good or bad lie. And in the more 'civilized' contexts where women are replaced and excluded from magico-religious functions, adults who still live on storytelling become bums who spend their time feeding on lies, 'them big old lies we tell when we're jus' sittin' around here on the store porch doin' nothin'.' When Zora Neale Hurston came back to Eatonville, Florida, to collect old stories, her home folks proudly told her: 'Zora, you come to de right place if lies is what you want. Ah'm gointer lie up a nation'; or 'Now, you gointer hear lies above suspicion'; or else 'We kin tell you some lies most any ole time. We never run outer lies and lovin'.'[21] All right, let them call it lie, let us smile and call it lie too if that satisfies them, but 'let de lyin' go on!' For we do not just lie, we lie and love, we 'lie up a nation', and our lies are 'above suspicion'. How can they be otherwise when they derive their essence from that gift of God: speech? Speech, that active agent in our Mothers' magic; speech, which owes its fertilizing power to ... who else but the Mother of God?

The woman warrior: she who breaks open the spell

> Thought-Woman / is sitting in her room / and whatever she thinks about / appears. / She thought of her sisters, / . . . / and together they created the Universe / . . . / Thought-Woman, the spider, / named things and / as she named them / they appeared (Leslie Marmon Silko)[22]

The touch infinitely delicate awakens, restores them to life, letting them surge forth in their own measures and their own rhythms. The touch infinitely attentive of a fairy's wand, a woman's voice, or a woman's hand, which goes to meet things in the dark and pass them on without deafening, without extinguishing in the process. Intense but gentle, it holds words out in the direction of things or lays them down nearby things so as to call them and breathe new life into them. Not to capture, to chain them up, nor to mean. Not to instruct nor to discipline. But to kindle that zeal which hibernates within each one of us. 'Speech may create peace, as it may destroy it. It is like fire,' wrote A. Hampaté Bâ. 'One ill-advised word may start a war just as one blazing twig may touch off a great conflagration . . . Tradition, then, confers on . . . the Word not only creative power but a double function of saving and destroying.'[23] Her words are like fire. They burn and they destroy. It is, however, only by burning that they lighten.

From Africa to India and vice versa. Every woman partakes in the chain of guardianship and of transmission. Every griotte *who dies is a whole library that burns down.*

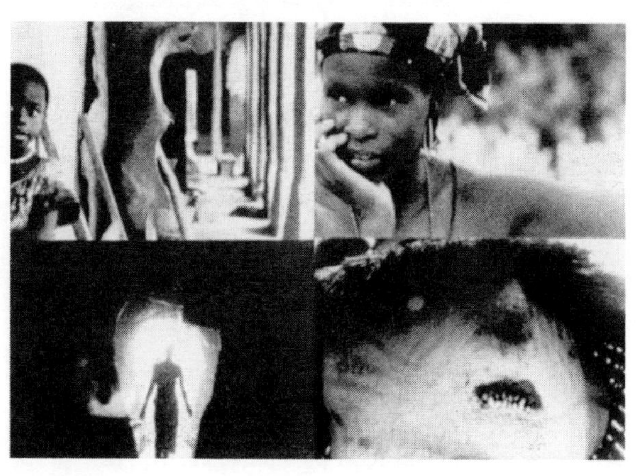

We fear heights, we fear the headless, the bottomless, and boundless . . . This is why we keep on doing violence to words: to tame and cook the wild raw, to adopt the vertiginously infinite.

Destroying and saving, therefore, are here one single process. Not two processes posed in opposition or in conflict. They would like to order everything around hierarchical oppositions. They would like to cut her power into endless opposing halves or cut herself from the Mothers' powers – setting her against either her mother, her godmother, her mother-in-law, her grandmother, her daughter, or her granddaughter. One of them has to be wicked so as to break the network of transmission. This is cleverly called jealousy among women, the jealousy of the woman who cannot suffer seeing her daughter or another woman take more pleasure in life than herself. For years and years, centuries and centuries, they have devoted their energies to breaking bonds and spreading discords and confusion. Divide and conquer. Mothers fighting mothers. Here is what an Indian witch has to say on 'white skin people / like the belly of a fish / covered with hair':

> . . . They see no life
> When they look
> they see only objects.
> . . . They fear
> They fear the world.
> They destroy what they fear.
> They fear themselves.
> . . . Stolen rivers and mountains

> the stolen land will eat their hearts
> and jerk their mouths from the Mother.
> The people will starve. [24]

These are excerpts of a story passed on by Leslie Marmon Silko. The story is the vision of a witch who, a long time ago, at a contest of witches from all the pueblos, 'didn't show off any dark thunder charcoals or red anthill beads' like the other witches, but only asked them to listen: 'What I have is a story . . . laugh if you want to / but as I tell the story / it will begin to happen.' Scanned by the refrain 'set in motion now / set in motion / to work for us' the story thus unfolds, naming as it proceeds the killing, the destruction, the foul deed, the loss of the white man, and with it, the doom of the Indian people. 'It isn't so funny . . . Take it back. Call that story back,' said the audience by the end of the story, but the witch answered: 'It's already turned loose / It's already coming. / It can't be called back.' A story is *not* just a story. Once the forces have been aroused and set into motion, they can't simply be stopped at someone's request. Once told, the story is bound to circulate; humanized, it may have a temporary end, but its effects linger on and its end is never truly an end. Who among us has not, to a certain extent, felt what George Ebers, for example, felt toward his mother's stories: 'When the time of rising came, I climbed joyfully into my mother's warm bed, and never did I listen to more beautiful fairy tales than at those hours. They became instinct with life to me and have always remained so ... It is a singular thing that actual events which happened in those early days have largely vanished from my memory, but the fairy tales I heard and secretly experienced became firmly impressed on my mind.'[25] The young beautiful fairy and the old ugly witch, remember, have the same creative power, the same decisive force of speech. As she names them, they appear ... The story tells us not only what might have happened, but also what *is happening* at an unspecified time and place. Whenever Ebers had the slightest doubt in mind, he would immediately appeal to his mother, for he thought 'she could never be mistaken and knew that she always told the truth'. Lying is not a mother's attribute. Or else, if lying is what you think she does, then she will 'never run outer lies and lovin''.

> When we Chinese girls listened to the adult talk-story, we learned that we failed if we grew up to be but wives or slaves. We could be heroines, swordswomen ... Night after night my mother would talk-story until we fell asleep. I couldn't tell where the stories left off and the dreams began, her voice the voice of the heroines in my sleep ... At last I saw that I too had been in the presence of great power, my mother talking-story ... She said I would grow up a

> wife and a slave, but she taught me the song of the warrior woman, Fa Mu Lan. I would have to grow up a warrior woman. (Maxine Hong Kingston)[26]

She fires her to achievement and she fires her with desire to emulate. She fires her with desire to emulate the heroines of whom she told and she fires her with desire to emulate the heroine who tells of the other heroines, 'I too had been in the presence of great power, my mother talking-story'. What is transmitted from generation to generation is not only the stories, but the very power of transmission. The stories are highly inspiring, and so is she, the untiring storyteller. She, who suffocates the codes of lie and truth. She, who loves to tell and retell and loves to hear them told and retold night after night again and again. Hong Kingston grows up a warrior woman and a warrior-woman-storyteller herself. She is the woman warrior who continues to fight in America the fight her mothers fought in China. Even though she is often 'mad at the Chinese for lying so much', and blames her mother for lying with stories, she happily *lets the lying go on* by retelling us her mother's 'lies' and offering us versions of her stories that can be called lies themselves. Her brother's version of a story, she admits it herself, 'may be better than mine because of its bareness, not twisted into designs'. Her brother, indeed, is no woman warrior-storyteller. Hong Kingston's apparent confusion of story and reality is, in fact, no confusion at all since it is an unending one; her parents often accuse her of not being able to 'tell a joke from real life' and to understand that Chinese 'like to say the opposite'. Even the events described by her relatives in their letters from China she finds suspect: 'I'd like to go to China and see those people and find out what's cheat story and what's not.' The confusion she experienced in her girlhood is the confusion we all experience in life, even when we think, as adults, that we have come up with definite criteria for the true and the false. What is true and what is not, and who decides so if we wish not to have this decision made *for* us? When, for example, Hong Kingston yells at her mother: 'You can't stop me from talking. You tried to cut off my tongue, but it didn't work', we not only know she is quite capable of telling 'fancy' from 'facts', we are also carried a step further in this differentiation by her mother's answer: 'I cut it to make you talk more, not less, you dummy.'[27] (Her mother has already affirmed elsewhere that she cut it so that her daughter would not be 'tongue-tied'.) The opening story of *The Woman Warrior* is a forbidden story ('No Name Woman') that begins with Hong Kingston's mother saying: 'You must not tell anyone what I am about to tell you.' Twenty years after she heard this story about her father's sister who drowned herself and her baby in the family well, not only has Hong Kingston broken open the spell cast upon her aunt by retelling the story – 'I alone devote pages of paper to her' – but she has done it in such a way as to reach thousands and thousands of listeners and readers. Tell it to the world. To preserve is to pass on, not to keep for oneself. A story told is a story bound to circulate. By telling her daughter not to tell it to anyone, the mother knew what she was supposed to say, for 'That's what Chinese say. We like to say the opposite.' She knew she was in fact the first before her daughter to break open the spell. The family cursed her, she who committed adultery and was such a spite suicide (the aunt); the men (her brothers) tabooed her name and went on living 'as if she had never been born'; but the women (Hong Kingston's mother and those who partook in this aunt's death) would have to carry her with(in) them for life and pass her on, even though they condemned her no less. For every woman is the woman of all women, and this one died first and foremost for being a woman. ('Now that you have started to menstruate', the mother warned her daughter, 'what happened to her could happen to you. Don't humiliate us.') Hong Kingston has, in her own way, retained many of the principles of her mother's storytelling. If, in composing with 'fancy' and 'fact', the latter knows when she should say 'white is white' and when she should say 'white is black' in referring to the same thing, her daughter also knows when to dot her i's and when not to. Her writing, neither fiction nor non-fiction, constantly invites the reader either to drift naturally from the realm of imagination to that of actuality or to live them both without ever being able to draw a clear line between them yet never losing sight of their differentiation. What Hong Kingston does *not* tell us about her mother but allows us to read between the lines and in the gaps of her stories reveals as much about her mother as what she *does* tell us about her. This, I feel, is the most 'truthful' aspect of her work, the very power of her storytelling. *The Woman Warrior* ends with a story Hong Kingston's mother told her, not when she was young, she says, 'but recently, when I told her I also talk-story'. The beginning of the story, which relates how the family in China came to love the theater through the grandmother's passion for it and her generosity, is the making of the mother. The ending of the story, which recalls one of the songs the poetess Ts'ai Yen composed while she was a captive of the barbarians and how it has been passed down to the Chinese, is the making of the daughter – Hong

Kingston herself. Two powerful woman storytellers meet at the end of the book, both working at strengthening the ties among women while commemorating and transmitting the powers of our foremothers. At once a grandmother, a poetess, a storyteller, and a woman warrior.

A cure and a protection from illness

> I grew up with storytelling. My earliest memories are of my grandmother telling me stories while she watered the morning-glories in her yard. Her stories were about incidents from long ago, incidents which occurred before she was born but which she told as certainly as if she had been there. The chanting or telling of ancient stories to effect certain cures or protect from illness and harm have always been part of the Pueblo's curing ceremonies. I feel the power that the stories still have to bring us together, especially when there is loss and grief. (Leslie Marmon Silko)[28]

Refresh, regenerate, or purify. Telling stories and watering morning-glories both function to the same effect. For years and years she has been renewing her forces with regularity to keep them intact. Such ritual ablutions – the telling and retelling – allow her to recall the incidents that occurred before she was born with as much certainty as if she had witnessed them herself. The words passed down from mouth to ear (one sexual part to another sexual part), womb to womb, body to body are the remembered ones. S/He whose belly cannot contain (also read 'retain') words, says a Malinke song, will succeed at nothing. The further they move away from the belly, the more liable they are to be corrupted. (Words that come from the MIND and are passed on directly 'from mind to mind' are, consequently, highly suspect . . .) In many parts of Africa, the word 'belly' refers to the notion of occult power. Among the Basaa of Cameroon, for example, the term *hu*, meaning (a human being's) 'stomach', is used to designate 'a thing whose origin and nature nobody knows', but which is unanimously attributed to women and their powers. A Basaa man said he heard from his fathers that 'it was the woman who introduced the *hu*' into human life. In several myths of the Basaa's neighboring peoples, *evu*, the equivalent of the Basaa's *hu*, is said to have requested that it be carried in the woman's belly at the time it first met her and to have entered her body through her sexual part. Thus associated with women, the *hu* or *evu* is considered both maleficent and beneficent. It is at times equated with devil and sorcery, other times with prophecy and anti-sorcery. S/He who is said to 'have a *hu*' is both feared and admired. S/He is the one who sees the invisible, moves with ease in the night-world as if in broad daylight, and is endowed with uncommon, exceptional intelligence, penetration, and intuition.[29] Woman and magic. Her power resides in her belly – Our Mother's belly – for her cure is not an isolated act but a total social phenomenon. Sorcery, according to numerous accounts, is hereditary solely within the matrilineal clan; and a man, in countless cases, can only become a sorcerer (a wizard) through the transmission of power by a sorceress (witch). He who understands the full power of woman and/in storytelling also understands that life is not to be found in the mind nor in the heart, but there where she carries it:

> I will tell you something about stories, [he said]
> They aren't just entertainment.
> Don't be fooled.
> They are all we have, you see,
> all we have to fight off
> illness and death.
> You don't have anything
> if you don't have the stories . . .
> He rubbed his belly.
> I keep them here [he said]
> Here, put your hand on it
> See, it is moving
> There is life here
> for the people.[30]

The story as a cure and a protection is at once musical,

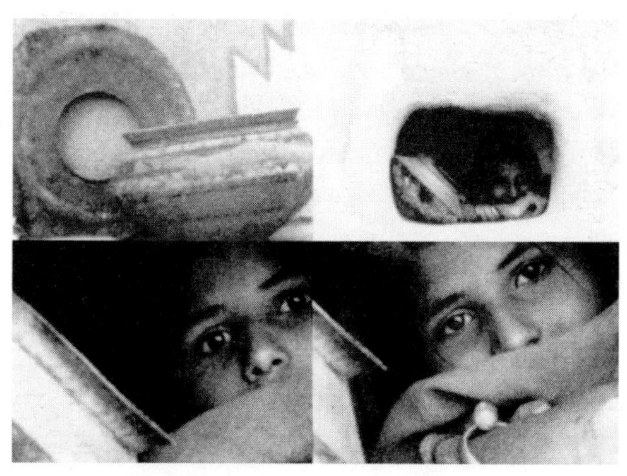

The story is older than my body, my mother's, my grandmother's. For years we have been passing it on so that it may live, shift, and circulate. So that it may become larger than its proper measure, always larger than its own in-significance.

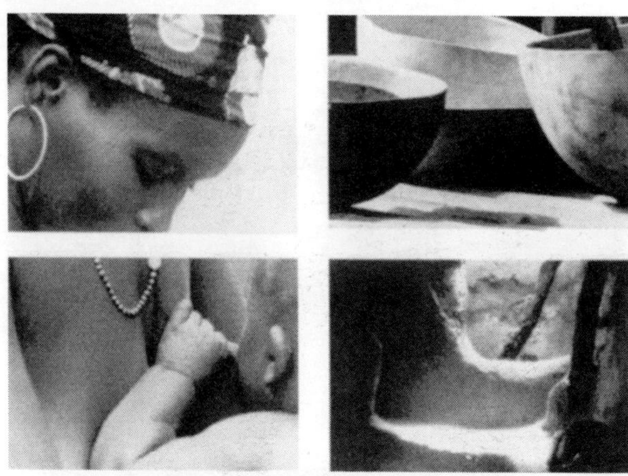

'Speech . . . creates a bond of coming-and-going which generares movement and rhythm . . . life and action'
(A. Hampaté Bâ)

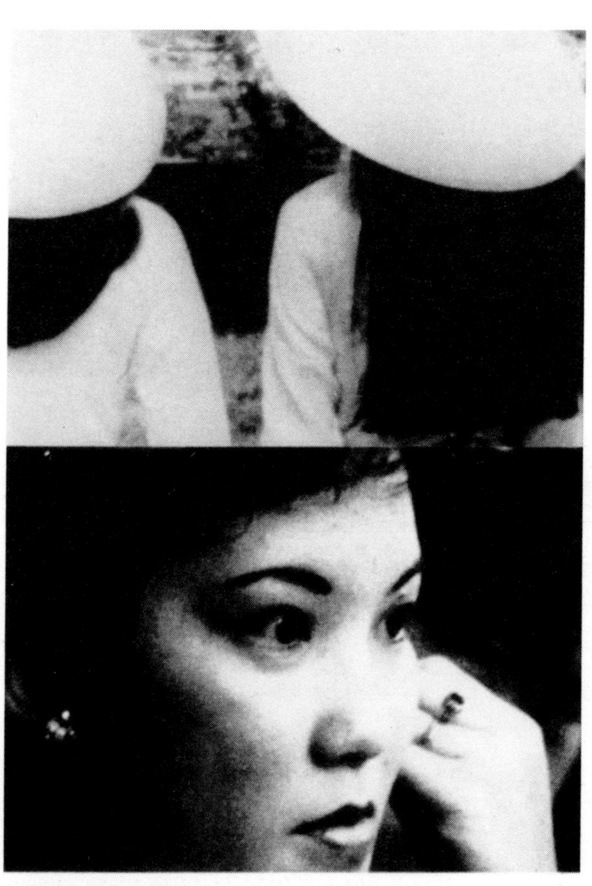

historical, poetical, ethical, educational, magical, and religious. In many parts of the world, the healers are known as the living memories of the people. Not only do they hold esoteric and technical knowledge, but they are also kept closely informed of the problems of their communities and are entrusted with all family affairs. In other words, they know everyone's story. Concerned with the slightest incident, they remain very alert to their entourage and heedful of their patients' talks. They derive their power from *listening* to the others and *absorbing* daily realities. While they cure, they take into them their patients' possessions and obsessions and let the latter's illnesses become theirs. Their actions imply a personal investment of which the healing technics form only a part and are a reflection. 'I see the patient's psychic life', many of them say, 'nothing is hidden from me'. Dis-ease breeds dis-ease; life engenders life. The very close relationship these healers maintain with their patients remains the determining factor of the cure. Curing means re-generating, for understanding is creating. The principle of healing rests on *reconciliation,* hence the necessity for the family and/or the community to cooperate, partake in, and witness the recovery, de-possession, regeneration of the sick. The act of healing is therefore a socio-cultural act, a collective, motherly undertaking. (Here, it is revealing to remember that male healers often claim to be wedded to at least two wives: a terrestrial one *and* a spiritual one. The spiritual wife or the 'woman spirit' protects the healer and is the source of his powers. She is the one who 'has knowledge' and from whom he seeks advice in all matters. When she becomes too demanding and too possessive, it is said that only one person can send her away: the healer's own mother.)[31] The storyteller, besides being a great mother, a teacher, a poetess, a warrior, a musician, a historian, a fairy, and a witch, is a healer and a protectress. Her chanting or telling of stories, as Marmon Silko notices, has the power of bringing us together, especially when there is sickness, fear, and grief. '"*When they look / they see only objects*", / They fear / they never stop fearing / but they see not fear the living thing. / They follow not its movements / for they fear not to fear. / "*They destroy what they fear. / They fear themselves.*" / They destroy the stories / let these be confused or forgotten / let these be only stories / They would like that . . .'

> Stolen rivers and mountains
> the stolen land will eat their hearts
> and jerk their mouths from the Mother.
> The people will starve.[32]

'Tell it the way they tell it'

It is a commonplace for those who consider the story to be just a story to believe that, in order to appropriate the 'traditional' storytellers' powers and to produce the same effects as theirs, it suffices to 'look for the structure of their narratives'. *See them as they see each other*, so goes the (anthropological) creed. 'Tell it the *way* they tell it instead of imposing *our* structure', they repeat with the best of intentions and a conscience so clear that they pride themselves on it. Disease breeds disease. Those who function best within definite structures and spend their time structuring their own or their peers' existences must obviously 'look for' that which, according to their 'findings' and analyses, is supposed to be 'the structure of their [the storytellers'] narratives'. What we 'look for' is un/fortunately what we shall find. The anthropologist, as we already know, does not *find* things; s/he *makes* them. And makes them up. The structure is therefore not something given, entirely external to the person who structures, but a projection of that person's way of handling realities, here narratives. It is perhaps difficult for an analytical or analytically trained mind to admit that recording, gathering, sorting, deciphering, analyzing and synthesizing, dissecting and articulating are already 'imposing our [/a] structure', a structural activity, a structuring of the mind, a whole mentality. (Can one 'look for a structure' without structuring?) But it is particularly difficult for a dualistic or dualistically trained mind to recognize that 'looking for the structure of their narratives' already involves the separation of the structure from the narratives, of the structure from that which is structured, of the narrative from the narrated, and so on. It is, once more, as if form and content stand apart; as if the structure can remain fixed, immutable, independent of and unaffected by the changes the narratives undergo; as if a structure can only function as a standard mold within the old determinist schema of cause and product. Listen, for example, to what a man of the West had to say on the form of the story:

> Independent of the content which the story carries, and which may vary from history to nonsense, is the form of the story which is practically the same in all stories. The content is varied and particular, the form is the same and universal. Now there are four main elements in the form of each story, viz. the beginning, the development, the climax, and the end.[33]

Just like the Western drama with its four or five acts. A drama whose naïve claim to universality would not fail to make this man of the West our laughingstock. 'A good story', another man of the West asserted, 'must have a beginning that rouses interest, a succession of events that is orderly and complete, a climax that forms the story's point, and an end that leaves the mind at rest.'[34] No criteria other than those quoted here show a more thorough investment of the Western mind. *Get them* – children, storybelievers – *at the start; make your point* by ordering events to a definite *climax*; then *round out to completion*; descend to a rapid close – not one, for example, that puzzles or keeps them puzzling over the story, but one that *leaves the mind at rest*. In other words, to be 'good' a story must be built in conformity with the ready-made idea some people – Western adults – have of reality, that is to say, a set of prefabricated schemata (prefabricated by whom?) they value out of habit, conservatism, and ignorance (of other ways of telling and listening to stories). If these criteria are to be adopted, then countless non-Western stories will fall straight into the category of 'bad' stories. Unless one makes it up or invents a reason for its absence, one of these four elements required always seems to be missing. The stories in question either have no development, no climax that forms the story's point, or no end that leaves the mind at rest. (One can say of the majority of these stories that their endings precisely refute such generalization and rationale for they offer no security of this kind. An example among endless others is the moving story of 'The Laguna People' passed on by Marmon Silko, which ends with a little girl, her sister, and the people turning into stone while they sat on top of a mesa, after they had escaped the flood in their home village below. Because of the disquieting nature of the resolution here, the storytellers [Marmon Silko and her aunt] then add, as a compromise to the fact-oriented mind of today's audience: 'The story ends there. / Some of the stories / Aunt Susi told / have this kind of ending. / There are no explanations.'[35] There is no point [to be] made either.) 'Looking for the structure of *their* narratives' so as to 'tell it the way *they* tell it' is an attempt at remedying this ignorance of other ways of telling and listening (and, obviously, at re-validating the nativist discourse). In doing so, however, rare are those who realize that what they come up with is not 'structure of *their* narratives' but a reconstruction of the story that, at best, makes a number of its functions appear. Rare are those who acknowledge the unavoidable transfer of values in the 'search' and admit that 'the attempt will remain largely illusory: we shall never know if the other, into whom we cannot, after all, dissolve, fashions from the elements of [her/]his social existence a synthesis exactly superimposable on that which we have worked out.'[36] The attempt will remain illusory as long as the controlled succession of certain mental operations which constitutes the structural activity is not made explicit and dealt with – not just mentioned. Life is not a (Western) drama of four or five acts. Sometimes it just drifts along; it may go on year after year without development, without climax, without definite beginnings or endings. Or it may accumulate climax upon climax, and if one chooses to mark it with beginnings and endings, then everything has a beginning and an ending. There are, in this sense, no good or bad stories. In life, we usually don't know when an event is occurring; we think it is starting when it is already ending; and we don't see its in/significance. The present, which saturates the total field of our environment, is often invisible to us. The structural activity that does not carry on the cleavage between form and content but emphasizes the interrelation of the material and the intelligible is an activity in which structure should remain an unending question: one that speaks him/her as s/he speaks it, brings it to intelligibility.

'The story must be told. There must not be any lies'

'Looking for the structure of their narratives' is like looking for the pear shape in Erik Satie's musical composition *Trois Pièces en Forme de Poire* (Three Pieces in a Pear Shape). (The composition was written after Satie met with Claude Debussy, who criticized his music for 'lacking of form'.) If structure, as a man (R. Barthes) pertinently defines it, is 'the residual deposit of duration', then again, rare are those who can handle it by letting it come, instead of hunting for it or hunting it down, filling it with their own marks and markings so as to consign it to the meaningful and lay claim to it. *'They see no life / When they look / they see only objects.'* The ready-made idea they have of reality prevents their perceiving the story as a living thing, an organic process, a way of life. What is taken for stories, only stories, are fragments of/in life, fragments that never stop interacting while being complete in themselves. A story in Africa may last three months. The storyteller relates it night after night, continually, or s/he starts it one night and takes it up again from that point three months later. Meanwhile, as the occasion arises, s/he may start on yet another story. Such is life . . . :

> The gussucks [the Whites] did not understand the story; they could not see the way it must be told, year after year as the old man had done, without lapse or silence . . .
> 'It began a long time ago', she intoned steadily . . . she did not pause or hesitate; she went on with the story, and she never stopped . . . [37]

'Storyteller', from which these lines are excerpted, is another story, another gift of life passed on by Marmon Silko. It presents an example of multiple storytelling in which story and life merge, the story being as complex as life and life being as simple as a story. The story of 'Storyteller' is the layered making of four storytellers: Marmon Silko, the woman in the story, her grandmother, and the person referred to as 'the old man'. Except for Marmon Silko who plays here the role of the coordinator, each of these three storytellers has her/his own story to live and live with. Despite the differences in characters or in subject matter, their stories closely interact and constantly overlap. The woman makes of her story a continuation of her grandmother's, which was left with no ending – the grandmother being thereby compelled to bear it (the story) until her death, her knees and knuckles swollen grotesquely, 'swollen with anger' as she explained it. She bore it, knowing that her granddaughter will have to bear it too: 'It will take a long time,' she said, 'but the story must be told. There must not be any lies.' Sometime after her death, exactly when does not matter, when the time comes, the granddaughter picks up the story where her grandmother left it and carries it to its end accordingly, the way 'it must be told'. She carries it to a certain completion by bringing in death where she intends to have it in her story: the white storeman who lied in her grandma's story and was the author of her parents' death would have to pay for his lies, but his death would also have to be of his own making. The listener/reader does not (have to) know whether the storeman in the granddaughter's story is the same as the one who, according to the grandmother, 'left right after that [after he lied and killed]' (hence making it apparently impossible for the old woman to finish her story). A storeman becomes *the* storeman, the man in the store, the man in the story. (The truthfulness of the story, as we already know, does not limit itself to the realm of facts.) Which story? *The* story. What grandma began, granddaughter completes and passes on to be further completed. As a storyteller, the woman (the granddaughter) does not directly kill; she decides when and where that storeman will find death, but she does not carry out a hand-to-hand fight and her murder of him is no murder in the common, factual sense of the term: all she needs to do is set in motion the necessary forces and let them act on their own.

> They asked her again, what happened to the man from the Northern Commercial Store. 'He lied to them. He told them it was safe to drink. But I will not lie . . . I killed him', she said, 'but I don't lie.'

When she is in jail, the Gussuck attorney advises her to tell the court *the truth*, which is that it was an accident, that the

'I intended that he die. The story must be told as it is.

'Civilization is not mere advance in technology and in the material aspects of life. We should remember it is an abstract noun and indicates a state of living and not things.' (C. Rajagopalachari)

Storytelling: her words set into motion the forces that lie dormant in things and beings

storeman ran after her in the cold and fell through the ice. That's all what she has to say – then 'they will let [her] go home. Back to [her] village.'

> She shook her head. 'I will not change the story, not even to escape this place and go home. I intended that he die. The story must be told as it is.' The attorney exhaled loudly; his eyes looked tired. 'Tell her that she could not have killed him that way. He was a white man. He ran after her without a parka or mittens. She could not have planned that.'[38]

When the helpful, conscientious (full-of-the-white-man's-complex-of-superiority) attorney concludes that he will do 'all [he] can for her' and will explain to the judge that 'her mind is confused', she laughs out loud and finally decides to tell him the story anew: '*It began a long time ago . . .*' (my italics). He says she could not have killed that white man because, again, for him the story is just a story. But Thought-Woman, Spider-Woman is a fairy and a witch who protects her people and tells stories to effect cures. As she names Death, Death appears. The spell is cast. Only death gives an ending to the stories in 'Storyteller'. (The old man's story of the giant bear overlaps with the granddaughter's story and ends the moment the old man – the storyteller – dies.) Marmon Silko as a storyteller never loses sight of the difference between truth and fact. Her naming retains the accuracy and magic of our grandmothers' storytelling without ever confining itself to the realm of factual naming. It is accurate because it is at once extremely flexible and rigid, not because it wishes to stick to certain rules of correctness for reasons of mere conservatism (scholars studying traditional storytelling are often impressed by the storyteller's 'necessity of telling the stories correctly', as they put it). It is accurate because it partakes in the setting into motion of forces that lie dormant in us. Because, as African storytellers sing, 'the tongue that falsifies the word / taints the blood of [her/] him that lies.'[39] Because she who bears it in her belly cannot cut herself off from herself. Off from the bond of coming-and-going. Off from her great mothers.

'May my story be beautiful and unwind like a long thread ...' she recites as she begins her story. Here she chants the time-honored formula that opens the tales of Kabyle folksingers, but what she chants, in a way, is a variant of what her African *griotte*-sisters chant every time they set about composing on life: tell me so that I can tell my hearers what I have heard from you who heard it from your mother and your great mother ... Each woman, like each people, has her own way of unrolling the ties that bind. Storytelling, the oldest form of building historical consciousness in community, constitutes a rich oral legacy, whose values have regained all importance recently, especially in the context of writings by women of color. She who works at un-learning the dominant language of 'civilized' missionaries also has to learn how to un-write and write anew. And she often does so by re-establishing the contact with her foremothers, so that living tradition can never congeal into fixed forms, so that life keeps on nurturing life, so that what is understood as the Past continues to provide the link for the Present and the Future. As our elder Lao Tzu says, 'Without allowance for filling, a valley will run dry; / Without allowance for growing, creation will stop functioning.' Tradition as on-going commitment, and in women's own terms. The story is beautiful, because or therefore it unwinds like a thread. A long thread, for there is no end in sight. Or the end she reaches leads actually to another end, another opening, another 'residual deposit of duration'. Every woman partakes in the chain of guardianship and of transmission – in other words, of creation. Every *griotte* who dies is a whole library that burns down. Tell it so that they can tell it. So that it may become larger than its measure, always larger than its own in/significance. In this horizontal and vertical vertigo, she carries the story on, motivated at once by the desire to finish it and the necessity to remind herself and others that 'it's never finished'. A lifetime story. More than a lifetime. One that will be picked up where it is left; when, it does not matter. For the time is already set. 'It will take a long time . . .' the grandmother ends; 'it began long ago . . .' the granddaughter starts. The time is set, she said; not in terms of when exactly but of what: what exactly must be told, and how. 'There must not be any lies.' Like Maxine Hong Kingston who decided to tell the world the forbidden story of her tabooed aunt, the 'No Name Woman', Marmon Silko's granddaughter-storyteller opens the spell cast upon her people, by re-setting into motion what was temporarily delayed in the story of her grandmother. The burden of the story-truth. She knew that during her own lifetime the moment would come when she would be able to assume her responsibility and resume the grandmother's interrupted story trajectory. She killed the one who lied to her people, who actively participated in the slow extinction of her race. She killed Him. She killed the white storeman in 'her story' which is not 'just a story': 'I intended that he die. The story must be told as it is.' To ask, like the white attorney, whether the story she tells makes any sense, whether it is factually possible, whether it is true or not is to cause confusion by an incorrect question. Difference here is not understood as difference. Her (story) world remains therefore irreducibly foreign to Him. The man can't hear it the way she means it. He sees her as victim, as unfortunate object of hazard. 'Her mind is confused', he concludes. She views herself as the teller, the un-making subject, the agent of the storeman's death, the moving force of the story. She didn't know when exactly she would be able to act in concordance with fate (she is also fate), but she planned and waited for the ripe moment to come, so that what appeared as an accident was carefully matured. Her sense of the story overflows the boundaries of patriarchal time and truth. It overflows the notion of story as finished product ('just a story') – one neatly wrapped, that rounds off with a normative finale and 'leaves the mind at rest'. Marmon Silko's 'Storyteller' keeps the reader puzzling over the story as it draws to a close. Again, truth does not make sense. It exceeds measure: the woman storyteller sees her vouching for it as a defiance of a whole system of the white man's lies. She values this task, this responsibility over immediate release (her being freed from imprisonment through the attorney's advice), over immediate enlightenment and gratification (vengeance for the sake of vengeance). Even if the telling condemns her present life, what is more important is to (re-)tell the story as she thinks it should be told; in other words, to maintain the difference that allows (her) truth to live on. The difference. He does not hear or see. He cannot give. Never the given, for there is no end in sight.

> There are these stories that just have to be told in the same way
> the wind goes blowing across the mesa
> – Leslie Marmon Silko, 'Stories and Their Tellers'

A BEDTIME STORY

Once upon a time,
an old Japanese legend
goes as told
by Papa,
an old woman traveled through
many small villages
seeking refuge for the night.
Each door opened
a sliver
in answer to her knock
then closed.
Unable to walk
any further
she wearily climbed a hill
found a clearing
and there lay down to rest
a few moments to catch
her breath.

The village town below
lay asleep except
for a few starlike lights.
Suddenly the clouds opened

and a full moon came into view
over the town.
The old woman sat up
turned toward
the village town
and in supplication
called out
Thank you people
of the village,
if it had not been for your
kindness
in refusing me a bed
for the night
these humble eyes would never
have seen this
memorable sight.

Papa paused, I waited.
In the comfort of our
hilltop home in Seattle
overlooking the valley,
I shouted
'That's the END?'
– Mitsuye Yamada, *Camp Notes*

Endnotes

1. Theresa Hak Kyung Cha, *Dictee* (New York: Tanam Press, 1982), p. 133.
2. Maxine Hong Kingston, *The Woman Warrior* (1975, rpt. New York: Vintage Books, 1977), p. 235.
3. Herman Harrell Horne, *Story-telling, Questioning and Studying* (New York: Macmillan, 1917), pp. 23-24.
4. *Dictee*, p. 123.
5. Gayl Jones, *Corregidora* (New York: Random House, 1975), p. 9.
6. Ibid., p. 184.
7. *Dictee*, p. 106.
8. Ibid., p. 130.
9. Horne, p. 34.
10. Katherine Dunlap Cather, *Educating by Story-telling* (New York: World Book Company, 1926), pp. 5-6.
11. Clark W. Hetherington, introduction in ibid., pp. xiii-xiv.
12. Anna Birgitta Rooth, *The Importance of Storytelling: A Study Based on Field Work in Northern Alaska* (Uppsala, Sweden: Almqvist & Wiksell, 1976), p. 88.
13. A. Hampaté Bâ, 'The Living Tradition', *General History of Africa, I. Methodology and African Prehistory*, ed. J. Ki Zerbo (UNESCO, Heineman, Univ. of California Press, 1981), p. 167.
14. Froebel quoted in Horne, p. 29.
15. *Dictee*, p. 150.
16. Quoted in Horne, p. 30.
17. Leslie Marmon Silko, 'Aunt Susie', *Storyteller* (New York: Seaver Books, 1981), p. 4.

18 Marcel Griaule, *Conversations with Ogotemmêli* (1965, rpt. New York: Oxford Univ. Press, 1975), pp. 26, 138-39.

19 Bâ, 'The Living Tradition', pp. 170-71.

20 On the part played by women in religious cults and their powers, see Robert Briffault, *The Mothers* (1927, rpt. New York: Atheneum, 1977), especially the chapter on 'The Witch and the Priestess', pp. 269-88.

21 Zora Neale Hurston, *Mules and Men*, excerpts in *I Love Myself*, ed. A. Walker (Old Westbury, N.Y.: Feminist Press, 1979), pp. 85, 93, 89.

22 Leslie Marmon Silko, *Ceremony* (New York: Viking Press, 1977), p. 1.

23 Bâ, 'The Living Tradition', p. 171.

24 *Ceremony*, pp. 132-38, or *Storyteller*, pp. 130-37.

25 Quoted in Cather, p. 22.

26 *The Woman Warrior*, pp. 23-24.

27 Ibid., pp. 189, 237, 240, 235.

28 *Ceremony*, back cover page.

29 For more information on the *hu* and its relation to women, see Meinrad P. Hebga, *Sorcellerie – Chimère dangereuse . . . ?* (Abidjan, Ivory Coast: INADES, 1979), pp. 87-115, 258-65.

30 *Ceremony*, p. 2.

31 Maurice Dorès, *La Femme Village* (Paris: L'Harmattan, 1981), pp. 20-25.

32 *Ceremony*, pp. 132-38.

33 Horne, p. 26.

34 E. P. St. John, *Stories and Story-telling*, quoted in Horne, p. 26.

35 *Storyteller*, pp. 38-42.

36 Claude Lévi-Strauss, *The Scope of Anthropology*, tr. S. Ortner Paul & R. A. Paul (1967, rpt. London: Jonathan Cape, 1971), p. 14.

37 *Storyteller*, pp. 31-32.

38 Ibid.

39 Bâ, 'The Living Tradition', p. 172.

Images

Production photographs by Jean-Paul Bourdier.